Happiness,
A Strange Bird

Patrice Pinette

Cover Painting by
Joan Hanley

2025
Bee Monk Press

These poems explore our quest for happiness—at times misguided, occasionally lucky, bitterly disappointing, or, at best, even blessed. The fleeting nature of happiness leads us to consider the inevitability of change and, if possible, to identify that which abides. While the poems address such themes as intimacy and distance, the colorful threads that bind us to the world and each other, they also present happiness as an awakening, arising from within rather than circumstance.

Celebrating the power of art and language to transform our experience, this collection offers an imaginative approach to the timeless search for the elusive, yet universal, gift of happiness.

For Gary

CONTENTS

Happiness, a Strange Bird	1
Blue Door	2
Of One Mind	3
Dark Energy	4
Out of Nowhere	6
As If	7
Night Vision	8
Heavy Light	10
Blue is a Being	11
Pure Honey	12
The Almond Croissant	13
On the Road to Emmaus	14
Vessels	15
The Story	16
It Dawns on You	17
An Early Lesson	19
Jonah's Camera	20
Peaches	21
Magnolia in a Killing Frost	22
First Snow	23
Don't Hate Winter	24
Looking Back	25
Owl	26
Seven Horses	27
Anima Mundi	28
Gingko	29
Balance is a Myth	30
Fantasy Bites the Tail of the Living	32
The World	33
Stained Glass	35
Embracing Solitude	36
Venus on Holiday	37

When my First Husband…	38
Down from Temple Mountain	40
Choreography	41
White Field	42
Blood Moon	43
Red	44
Rose Garden	45
Stones into Bread	46
Willard Pond Sanctuary	47
Crescent Moon	48
Jupiter Rising	49
Bion's Concept of O	50
The Letter O	51
Years Before Calamity	53
Halibut Point	54
Waiting between Worlds	55
In the Name of the Breeze	56
Birch	57
Feeding the Fire	58
Dublin Lake	59
Stitches	60
A Bridge	61
Arc	62
Peony	63
Pregnancy During a Pandemic	64
The Red Thread	65
Strawberries under the Snow	66
Raw Materials	67
Your Security has been Breached	68
Scarecrow in the Blessed Field	71
Bundles	72
Fields	73
Thorndike Pond	74
Late	75

Indra's Net	76
Equanimity	77
Chalice	78
Adam and Eve	79
Eve Speaking	80
Apple Tree	81
One Light at a Time	83
To Make Your Own Map	84
Chameleon's Manifesto	86
The Bookshop	87
Blue Banana	88
The Hiker	89
The Art of Falling	90
Magnetic Storm	91
Finger Painting	94
Brushwork	95
Chauvet Cave	96
Ideal Company	98
Fresh Figs	99
Peonies, a Bouquet	100
At the End of the Dying Day	101
Here	102
I would like to be a friend of silence	103
Bio	104
Acknowledgments	105
Gratitudes	106

Life is a spell so exquisite that everything conspires to break it.

Emily Dickinson

Happiness, a Strange Bird

Waking up without a cloud,
your heart has a feathery feeling,
playful even, could take to the sky,
but happiness is a strange bird
and builds her nest in dangerous
places. Also prone to illusion,
she attacks the window as if
her reflection is an enemy
come to steal her territory.
Or, seeing an idyllic landscape
in the glass, the morning sky
robin's egg blue, is stunned
when she tries to pass through.

Blue Door

Sometimes it is simple as opening an envelope:
What appears to be two dimensions becomes three.

Sky seen through trees—a blue door in the woods
opens us. Mushrooms are portals.

Have you too stepped through a door the rain made?
Other doors revolve. Like green ones in the waves.

You may think water will never break. But then it does—
and you push against it and it keeps opening

if you care to step out—
into the lobby. If not, you may continue going

in circles as others arrive with their luggage,
push lightly on the glass and disappear.

Of One Mind

In solidarity, it's said
we are of one mind.
Let one mind also mean
you feel solid yourself.
Inwardly united: separate
states forgo their boundaries
and their bickering. For a vision.
A new country crystallized.
A singularity, not the kind
of infinite density, rather a body
illumined by a single source.
A kind and joyous quiet settles.
Speaker listens. Listener breathes.
Single minded: the point
of departure and return.
An island in the green sea
touched by tides on every side,
abiding. One bridge across
the swell. The mind, at one
with the heart, arrowed
and arrested, still in love.

Dark Energy

Once we counted until we slept
the countless flames, sky-candles lit,
some falling towards us
in celebration of the world's birthday—
a few blown out by wind and wishes
against the blue-black table cloth.
Now the world grows old, or we have,
and the sky, no longer comforting,
scatters its silver—all lights racing away
from each other and from us, faster and faster
leaving black holes between the stars.

~

Something more or less than emptiness
flings galaxies away from each other.
Each star, like us, is animated not just in light
of its beginning, but by its endless drift.

Cold, inconceivable—our night vaster than before!
The mind numbs, but still dreams in pictures:
torn or stretched—heaven's dress.
Who or what will it reach and cover
beyond this universe, but into no other?

Arms reach around the globe, but the soul contracts.
Someone forgets to call, another feels left out.
Supernovas float, motherless, away.
We've grown apart, we say. Or, *she never really cared*.
We learn to live with distance.

~

I sleep beside my best friend, and sail,
for practice, into oblivion. Each night
one or the other of us wakes to keep watch,
but unable to steer our small boat at will,

senses the stars on their cosmic wheel,
their facets ground smooth and polished,
clocking the meridians and turning us towards day.
Silhouettes of hills crowned with first light. Clouds
streaked red dissipate, dreams dissolve. The hills:
waves, translucent green, surge into the harbor,
flooding the heart.

Out of Nowhere

A white flower comes to me
Why now
empty of dreams

The small flower lit from within
like a star indifferent   and yet

out of nothing it appears
over the earth of me
on a moonless night

As If

She was cold. I grew colder.
My resentment, many-faceted
felt beautiful. A diamond
that cost me.

I don't need to mention
the years. Not a lifetime
passed when she wrote:
"We could still have tea, yes?"

What could I say?
We set a time,
as if *this* time could
undo the other.

I'll tell you what she said,
what I said and so on,
like two old friends.
Into the silence between her question

and my answer, an epic rain fell.
At the next table, a religious lady
spoke about mercy as if
we were born to it.

Night Vision / Black Mirror
*A scrying mirror made of obsidian
is used in divination to see into the future.*

I

We want to see through
the dark

but breath fogs the glass
and the house falls

silent. What gap
between the stars

can we fill?
Love only knows

and hushes skin to skin
the question.

We would divine
lighter than air

or song, some answer—
spacious yet pointed

to meet the mark.
Our fortune fixed

in a scrying mirror:
its holy well

of quiet water
black and deepening.

II

To see what you can see,
take transparency,

your window to the world
as it is.

But to see what is not
yet—look into the dark

stone: obsidian.
In its black star, others

flicker and go out.
In deepest space

new lights spawn
as you look in,

careful not to catch
your own eye in the glass,

mistaking it—as once you did—
for an alien spirit

come to tell your fortune,
his gaze empty

as a fallen cup.

Heavy Light

The heavier the object, the more it drags on time.
Stephen Hawking

Tonight, heavyhearted, all thoughts bear down.
Dreams descend—the body drops anchor, immobile
when it's time to cry out. Nothing weighs less than fire,
      always making light.

A physicist tells us time travel is possible, and don't we know,
projecting back (and back again) to the café where we met,
returning to the future in those same seats.
      Then he explains the field of waves

coming and going: approaching, an object looks blue,
he said, and leaving shifts to red. Wait alone at the station
until love appears, out of the blue—then (remember!)
      the back of her red dress as she climbs aboard.

Sometimes we don't know if we're coming or going
and stand still, before the tide turns, the sky streaked
with lavender and deep purple clouds.
      It's not life itself whose primary principle is water,

as Thales proposed, but time, the river, flowing at different speeds.
Because it slows and quickens, because it falls over the ledge
gouging canyons from solid stone, because gravity, great maestro,
      changes the tempos, you take my hand too late

and leave too soon. What can we know about fate?
Is ending grave or graceful? Hours drag, fly, and lurch.
      My memory of you is no heavier than light.

Blue is a Being

Eat the seed of blue and it grows in you.
                                        Karine Munk Finser

Am I awake or asleep?

Unworthiness a salt upon my tongue,
I kneel

as Blue draws near, a sphere of light
so tall I cannot see her face.
But her shoulders stretch wide—no wonder
they call them wings.

My words, blue swallows, dart across her deepening dress.

Not: *What ocean do you carry on your hip?*
What heaven do you hail from? What country,
sapphire, cerulean?

But: *Where does the moral world begin?*

Leaning over the earth in me, the birth of me,
she answers space with time: *not where but when inner*
and outer light are one…

My legs still pressed against the ground, my cheek upon her hem

until the dawn

Pure Honey

We take a detour on the long way
home. Still winter in Vermont,
we pass a roadside stand selling *Pure Honey*.
I wave to the beekeeper as we drive by.
His eyes reply—Who are you? Do I know you?
Another lover, I want to say—of the word *pure*.
Longing—for the sweet new life, the next life—
as in a dream: a man at the side of the road,
his little table set up with glass jars, amber,
gleaming, devotion of bees, hidden seeds—
a sting to the heart.

The Almond Croissant

The almond croissant was divine.
Then it wasn't. What was it?
The air damp, the baker downcast,
even the salt and sugar clashed.

I considered a fast. An apple. A pear.
A cookbook. How hard can it be to mix and roll,
fill and fold and bake?

Today I weigh desire against restraint.
Happiness falls like crumbs from a
perfect feast. It must have been a wedding,
the bride ecstatic.

Then, content. Later, restless.
Shelling almonds, measuring flour,
sugar, salt.

On the Road to Emmaus

The stranger
came close
to their question

his voice
rose gentle-strong
as dawn

amazed at twilight's sky
bending to touch
each one

the friends drew closer
still   evening star setting
into them

but not until he broke
bread did the companions
recognize him and love

the giver   sun rain earth vine
tasting the imperishable
crumb

Vessels
After the Kabbalah creation story

Full of divine light, the vessels
overflowed. Who knows why
those houses of sky became fragile.
Fated to fail, fall like stars. Like words
falling silent once sounding like music
of the spheres, like angels, fearless,
until shattered. This world inheritance:
the broken bits, the barely seen gleam
in all beings and things. Splinters,
fragments so beautiful the heart,
also broken, gathers them tenderly,
like wildflowers. Like pebbles,
like stories. Until the beginning
and the middle find in their ending
the seeds of what's to become
whole. We were there. Primordial.
When every part mattered. Meant
something. Scattered. Still here,
shards in hand, placed side by side,
as pieces of a puzzle, belonging.
Vessels of morning. How much heat
can we hold of god-sparks, as collectors
of essence, light-bearers casting shadows,
in awe of sun, source, the one? Timeless.
This light held and holding us together.

The Story

The woman first
to know

already risen
drenched in dew

felt dawn
unravel

the winding cloth
of waiting

her heart tuned
to the hour

silence
softens stone

opens
the latch

to birdsong

Mary!

she was the one

nearest what can't
be held

but whole

she rose again
to tell

It Dawns on You

You forget the scent of daffodils
until a fresh cut bouquet breathes
out yellow from twenty golden
throats. Listening, you lean in,
almost tasting inner spring.
These tender flowers have little
time to light vernal pools
or be carried inside to make morning
out of night fears...What are you
afraid of? Being seen, stung, too high
strung? Some thickets threaten
to keep light out or lock it in.
Early flowers may fall prey to killing
frost—if not blessed by April's thaw
in time to open. Dawning more radiant
than candles, clearer than stars lost
in time-travel: tunnels of daffodils
are given passage from buried to bright
by the same sun seated in every body:
Hidden spark—resplendent yellow,
fiery source of I am ready, impatiently
saying—Now: *shine*.

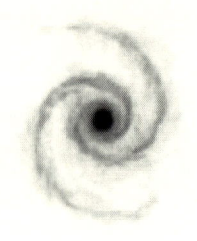

An Early Lesson

Today, Calum and I played
with a white ball. Later,
he played with his shadow
in the road—dark on dark,
waving back at him,
wearing ears of a little bear.
He can say a few words now—
hi and bye, mama, dada, ball,
bear, and bubbles, that cruel
game we play with the youngest,
blowing perfect, transparent
spheres sparkling with rainbows
that burst and disappear
at the lightest touch. To touch
is to destroy—such an early lesson.
Over and over the smile of delight.
Baffled. Then awaiting more—
still believing the exquisite
and fragile things we want
are meant for us to hold.

Jonah's Camera

One day, your son wants to photograph you
at the arboretum. He keeps his distance:
takes pictures of you in a tree and in a field
of marsh grass. You're dwarfed wherever
you stand.

Appearing ever smaller in the frame,
the focus is not you, but where you are
present, for a few moments, part of
the great branching of a weeping Beech
whose roots become your own.

In a dream, you can't tell who is lost,
who is looking. Did your young son wander
away, or did you? In a panic, you wake,
and he's already grown, studying perspective,
mechanics of near and far, zooming in, fading out.

Cezanne spoke of getting the right distance.
As a figure in the landscape, you can still find
your standpoint and take a light reading.
Only ideas have weight. You lighten as you age,
your water evaporates, and your fire begins to flow.

Said Merleau-Ponty of Cezanne: *To hold
is to hold at a distance.*

Peaches

Wild sun and wild trees
in the orchard that morning
ripe with sweetness bursting to be bitten
by Ariana, gold and pink peach-skin,
a soft sun-made shade in a dawn stamped early
with dew and delight.

Once paradise transplanted here—to trespass,
I hardly dared, but for my daughter, why not?
Summer light without a bonnet, a shine
without a shadow, sheer pleasure I wanted for her,
this taste of first days discovered, soft and succulent,
wind stirred and leaf lifted, this instant holding
like a gift for later. I don't mean canning. I mean we can,
she can, feel this good. Exquisite blush—golden rose,
free, all free—no coins, no owner, no grocer,
just Ari and me and the trees.

Who knew a peach could be Eden.
I felt the flame of the sword—not yet lifted
over the gate. Privilege of everything offered,
taken as if no end to ripening…not yet
underfoot the rotten ones, the flies,
the time.

Magnolia in a Killing Frost

*It was a flower / upon which April / had descended from the skies!
How bitter / a disappointment!*
                                William Carlos Williams

I wanted to climb into flowering branches
and watch the dancers shake their ankle bells:
soft white skirts twirling, the girls' hair garlanded and loose,
the boys' white pants rolled, white sleeves flapping as they circled
barefoot to the tambourine, ribbons weaving over and under
whatever wind was blowing.

Later, I slept, as frost pressed and pinched, then rose stiffly
to the tree, spring-fed and sun-bestowed—
I'd felt untimely warmth a gift myself, and miracle enough
to lift my heart again. But my face rose and fell among the leaves,
where bird-blossoms bloomed too soon and perfectly:
all ice. From pink petals to rusted rouge,

then cracked and brown as leather. Can joy be premature, dependent
on a thing like weather? Seasonless. Lichen's blue-gray scales
on speckled granite. The world grew older overnight, I nearly said.
But that wasn't right. I could take it in stride, and bent to daffodils
that survived the night.

First Snow

After a mild season, cold clouds
darken the hills, deep purple
against gray light. With the first
snowfall, the old world disguised,
it's easier to fall away from the known.
A Zen teacher told his student to go
into the mountain and wither away
like the grasses. Why starve with half
a handful of rice, if not to live
in the neighborhood of death long
enough to grasp life? At first
scent of snow, step off the ledge
of autumn. What will you bring back
from the storm? A dream of friends
who'd had enough of sorrow—
they lay down under a blizzard
of petals, or over the frozen pond,
or placed their cheek against the last
page of their last book and were gone.

Don't Hate Winter

Sunday morning quiet, no cars yet, but quieter than that:
what my eyes track of snowfall transfers like cotton
to my ears. I'm still as stone, inside a paperweight and safe,
while outside the glass, the world is shaken to white pieces.

You took a photograph once: "Dead Bird on Snow,"
lifeless, but perfect in every other way. Beauty in any form
warms us—so don't hate winter, G. You know you can't fight cold
with cold. What we need is more fierce, more fire—more tea?

The snow slows, and forms emerge again. White sleeved spruce
and snow-coated bare branches bleached as fishbones.
Today's negative becomes positive: a scratch art sketch,
with light lines etched where dark is scraped away. Words pure,

but reversed, fly the wrong way—call it *stark*, *isolating*.
But inversed again—not only white on black, but warmth
on cold, your hand in mine. Freezing burns. January thaws.
The kettle whistles.

Looking Back

Looking straight ahead, you see
what you'd expect, but in the rear view
mirror the same trees gleam white-iced,
each fan of branches, a constellation
sparked by sunlight, flashes beside the road
behind me. Up ahead, gray woods stark
and still in New Hampshire winter.
But where I passed, now the past,
illumined by sun's slant, is numinous
as the life already lived. Trees, laden
with lights like fruits, hold a harvest
of hindsight. Their radiant dots connect
and disappear around the next curve
in the road, the next naked sparkle
of late winter, in my backward glance,
dazzling the ordinary, like memory.

Owl

Stepping out the kitchen door
to feel how cold and how far
can I walk today, I saw the owl.
It met from above my gaze
from below. We stared the way
that stops clocks and vision
goes blurry all around the edges
of the mind which has met the mark.
A center of the world the arrow reaches
with astonishment, fixed there.
Fixed and frozen I hardly moved
as owl's head swiveled around
and back returning always to fierce
stillness but for feathers ruffling.
I looked upon the gray stage and saw
the white mask a god inhabits.
Who are you, what message? Tell me
what to think. Our little neighborhood
aglow sadly, as leaves bud, spread,
fall, and years peel bark from bone.
The winters hunger, snow and sparkle.
How does the soul look from above?
Her eyes yellow as the moon.

Seven Horses

Six brown horses
with black tails
and one white
one standing apart
makes the moon rise
over the field
more beautiful tied
to earth tense
with rising when full
of wanting to fall
and falling on the neck
of the one white horse
tethered to moonlight

Anima Mundi
for CB

It was easy to climb up.
Closer to the sun seemed
better than giving in too soon
to shadows. And the wind
felt good in the company of birds.
Heart breaking in the branches
was hard to hear over the creaking,
rustling and swaying. I could cry
or snap. No one would know
what I saw or felt when it was time
to go back. I was gathering light
and saving sap—ripening gold
for myself alone. I sighed deep
as roots—to take in the breath
of the world. I know—world sounds
too grand and nothing like the man
and boy I go home to—you know
what I mean—I wanted my soul alive
as the live oak I nested in.
I'd drowned through rain to the end
of the wood. And now no wind or storm
could shake me down until I chose.
Freedom. My word as a woman stood.

Gingko

We were used to sharing visions
and dreams, matter of fact magic.
Invisible worlds no more fantastic
than what meets the eye: this eagle
circling, dark wings stroking the sky,
white feathers shining the sun back
to itself. Omen over the parking lot.
Don't think the river, the bird, the stars
don't know our designs. We vowed
we wouldn't let go our saffron yellow
until Gingko Biloba drops its leaves,
all at once. Prehistoric tree, living fossil,
stands with the dignity of a Chinese sage
following Tao's silent *now*.
How many levels of light fan out as rings
in the core? There was a time before rainbows.
A time to count beads on a string.
A Gingko leaf of patinaed bronze
to wear like a cross—where deep time
meets deep space. Unified. Don't be afraid.
Worlds have died before. And a multitude
of seeds sleep in the vaults of the masters.

Balance is a Myth

The scales are always tipped.
Lady Justice is tired
of weighing herself
and every grain of rice
against hunger. She dreams
of excess and its consequence,
beauty of equivalencies.
How gleaming the scales
when they've met their match.
Three small oranges to two
large apples. A feather
against a tear always causes
a tremor, joy and sorrow
fated to take turns, never
in balance, circling planets,
passing in the dark.
The sun lost a chunk
of itself today, and we fear
falling apart. In Babylonia
chaos was called Tiamat,
terrifying to the gods,
her offspring. They tried
to defeat her, using her
body to make the world
wildly beautiful. Still,
chaos couldn't die—
any more than silence
can't be found in the midst
of sound. Some equations
are futile. Spaciousness
and form, truth and lies,
music and noise. Always,

there will be a gorgeous voice
with emptiness at its core.
A heart that skips before
it sinks. A deluge of grief
against two dragonflies
mating on the breeze.

Fantasy Bites the Tail of the Living

There is no other way: myth is the wound
we leave in the time we have
               Eaven Boland

Who can draw the line between a snake
on the ground and its rattle in a dream?
At the tattoo and piercing parlor

a man works surrounded by snakes—
painted, beaded, beaten metal, carved
in wood, and coiled clay. Some float

in formaldehyde. He'd been in prison
and shed that skin. Ribbon, rattle, cobra,
wind around his arms, vigilant,

yet charmed. He speaks about symbols
(a flicker of silver on his split tongue)
and the way truth is forked.

The World

Perhaps 2000 year old
    Buddha
is tired of waking
in Afghanistan

Perhaps the tallest
    Buddha
has seen enough
camel dung

Perhaps desecrating
    Buddha's body
will comfort
Allah

Perhaps timeless
    Buddha
turns celestial cheek
when wooden one is blown away

sips Turkish coffee
    with Mohammed
even now

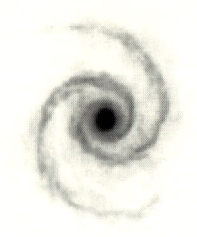

Stained Glass

The church turned into a conference room or was it
the other way around—the speaker wasn't sure himself
and his words about *living the symbolic life* sounded bland,
empty even to him, as his audience wandered away...

He wanted to inspire, point out that even the everyday
can be layered, multifaceted, enriched immeasurably,
imagination connecting in the deepest way with being,
ourselves, a little universe—take canning peaches for example,
it's a Sunday and suddenly it's Eden's perfect peaches
you are peeling, and the light on your hands is Vermeer's.

Then he walked around the edges of the sanctuary
looking at the stained-glass windows across the quiet space,
and not one face in them was pale but on fire, as the sun
that fell through Mary kept falling and falling
on the smooth gray stones, and the sleeves of the intellectual
fell limp and mild.

It's not about symbols, he thought, not really.
It's not about happiness either.
Loneliness is its own star.

Embracing Solitude

The holy man chose
silence

and love which loves to make of silence
praise

what else wells up
speechless

his old love struck down
only to rise late and lasting

quiet as dawn
birds clamor over

she stole over his desire
for nothing

more than God, but God
in her form of grace

eyes questioning
lips awed and open

like a vow
for him to take

Venus on Holiday

A green Caribbean sunset
is a parrot feather, a splash
of lime, an iced drink clinking.

When you turn away
it gets dark suddenly.
I cannot hear you thinking.

Tinkering with shells
and other discarded beauty
I leave the beach, suspicious
of the evening star.

When My First Husband Made Another Woman Pregnant

My teacher Adam spoke carefully.
His tongue held its place
emphasizing *s*, was pleased with itself
rolling those English *r's,*
bowed down to vowels.

He listened as intensely as he spoke,
entered other people's sorrows,
tasted other people's tears,
always had a wise word.
And why shouldn't he?
He read the stars.

He gave talks in Shalesbrook
by an open fire: on destiny and
folk souls and the temperament of Hamlet.
He was an expert on betrayal,
a spiritual man.

I can't remember how he fell.
He took a wound that would not heal.

It was then the woman from India
began to serve him.
Her dark eyes, her philosophy, her gentle
touch. Old man that he was,
he fell in love. Right under his wife's eyes.

They say it wasn't his first time.
He had a baby with someone else
a long time ago—in Scandinavia, I think.

So how could he be objective
when I told him about my husband?

What else could he say but—slow and deliberate,
each word a stone on my heart:
Let him go to her.

Down from Temple Mountain

Scattered fog in shreds
an eerie reminder
everything can be torn.

There is no way to understand
the occurrence of beauty

how it moves from the eye at dusk
to the ear at darkness.

And there is nothing you can say loudly
that will not be stronger
in a quiet voice
poised on the edge of the bed or

gazing into your closet
back turned to your lover
about how you failed.

To forgive yourself feels
impossible, so you don't forget.
You go on.

Study a book of Japanese art since 1945:

Red brushstroke across black background
the title also red—*Scream Against the Sky.*

And we who made the sky awful
now called *friend, ally.*

Choreography
after Winter Herons by Barry Lopez

The story bothered me—it was beautiful,
but didn't go anywhere other
than Colorado and New York.
There was a lover loving, as if
from a distance. He admired
her on and off the stage—a dancer.
The heart—where was it?
Landing on the island
between uptown and downtown
traffic in the middle of Manhattan
on a snowy evening: great blue herons
settling a while under the pale light
of streetlamps. White field
in the middle of the man
waiting, watching them wait
before shaking off their wings
and rising to an inaudible chord—
the whole troupe stroking the storm
as one, heading north.

White Field

You can look into the white field
    of a tulip and see only the dark
seeds of yourself

I have nothing to give, you say
    dwarfed by beauty

The poppy surrenders to light
    nods on its stem again and again

Why is it so difficult to believe in yourself
    long enough to serve the life
you ache to love?

There's a blizzard over your head
    a chance to catch stars on your tongue
as they fall

Blood Moon

Earth-shadow paints
her face red as sunset.
Blood Moon, rose wound,
memory-moon. Born
of violent impact moon,
molten moon, hardened,
reflecting sunlight moon
becomes nightlight,
back turned to the cold.
There's always someone
who wants to quell you,
wants you as conquest,
wants their flag visible
from your peak. Who
overshadows you?
Cuts deep. Leaves you
hidden behind a dark
mask. Just a phase.
Stay cool, sure of orbit.
Resilient, return to silver.
Notice beautiful, icy
space at your back inhabited
by other celestial bodies.
Commune with the stars.
Move out of the atmosphere
into everywhere.

Red

Chances are, as a water sign,
you prefer blue and green, maybe
the slate-gray of a stormy day.
You don't choose red. Some days,
though, red chooses you, appears
at the corner of your inner eye,
in the shape of a clenched fist.
Inescapably red. It's in*tense*,
as in desperate to hold on. Please don't
imagine the red fist of revolution.
OK, you already have. And who doesn't
need to rebel? Claim her freedom?
But before the revolt, there's the fist
of an iron grip. As in *get a grip*.
(Don't you say that to yourself
sometimes, before you lose it?)
You're a warrior, fighting invisible
foes. You catch your breath, hold on
to that too—must everyone and every-
thing dear depend on you? What if
you let go? What will crumble?
What will arise? Desire? Can you
take it? Taste it, be bold? Not to push
against, but to lean in, exude the life
force, the Yes, please! To make a mark
as the primordial ones made theirs,
leaving handprints, fingers spread
on cave walls. What would that sign
of presence look like now? Unafraid
to be seen, what about the one red dress
hidden in your closet? Hummingbirds
fly from one red flower to another.
Who wouldn't want that kind of bliss,
sunlit and ruby-bright as stained glass.

Rose Garden

Grace grows full
before giving way
to gravity—opening
for a brief time
the image of paradise.
Beholding roses
deepens intimacy
between the body
and the dream, between
lover and lost, between
the rosary and the rose cross.
At the heart of everything:
silence. Don't think
this is it. The lonely work
of the sun. White roses
uphold white gold at midday,
sunset stains some roses
red, bloodthirsty for
love. Blame brightness
for casting shadows.
They move through
the rose garden
on a long day in June.

Stones into Bread

You've waited until morning
to say something—what will it be?
Take note: are you glad or sad to be awake?
You can converse about the weather: the air cooler
and lighter. Yesterday, you felt loved. You loved.
Today, you can only imagine fields of snow,
the quiet erasure. But it's summer. And instead
of a pond or a stream, the shade garden has a river
of stones with a curved bridge like Monet's.
It's the deepest part of the garden, the center
around which the paths wind and pachysandra
and ajuga spread. One word leads to another.
You don't need to talk about bread, just eat it.
In this case, the loaf with three seeds—
flax: for forgetting you have nothing to say,
sesame: to remember the power of small,
and sunflower: to become like one
of those great transmitters tuned to the sky
to receive radio waves from the cosmos.
Be humble, stay with stones. Pocket one
not to soothe your worries, but to weigh
your words against. The mountain it came from
has already moved.

Willard Pond Sanctuary

They said to the one who lives in time,
Come. Let us look at you.
What have you done?
How many hours have slipped
away under your watch
unloved?

She fumbled for a match
as if flame could conjure
being. Few words passed
between them.

Speaking of the encounter later,
she said it was like swimming
in cool, smoothing waters
reflecting mountainsides
starting to turn—

and turning over to face the sky,
white clouds still blooming
and floating over the sanctuary
as storm-gray descends upon the hill
equally beautiful, equally belonging.

Crescent Moon

I imagine a strange peace—
no grief no struggle

In this quiet I am happy
from deep within out to my skin
A distance it takes years to fill

Don't think this sublime
containment is closed
It is open as the crescent moon is to the stars

as a book falls open to its reader
as lips part to begin a prayer

May you stand for once or at last
on holy ground that only looks
like loneliness

Jupiter Rising

Call it a god, a planet,
a big personality visiting
the cosmic houses, one by one,
until it arrives at yours,
bestowing a world of good
fortune. Expansive.
Magnanimous, the bliss
of belonging. Before you go
too far, sure you're invincible,
ready to test your good luck,
gambling your gold away—
decide to stay humble,
shining great affection
on strangers as on beloveds,
your heart bursting, like the pink
and white peonies—so gorgeous
and heavy, all they can do is bow.

Bion's Concept of O

O, representing the unknowable ultimate reality
                              Wilfred Bion

O—the hope of no other
name   no limiting word
no hold no holy no

Only—but circle
with no center and center
without fixed rim or reason

The only way he could say
that he couldn't say—O
the open wound the oak

of endless branching
Orion striding empty
dark to the boundless wave-welt

text-slashed, light-sashed
Prima before and after
Materia—daughter of O

The Letter O
after Wilfred Bion's tiger

One brush—one stroke
one circle divides the world:
the known and the unknown
        inside—outside
Which one is which?

      ***

In the circle dance of O
without hands take hands
whirling—stay still
        (but I'm dizzy!)
Grab hold of the tiger's tail

      ***

Will you be a stripe on the coat of the tiger?
Or will you meet the Tiger itself?
O my word—it's a tiger!
Carried on its back
fearless—the ink flying
from the ink stone

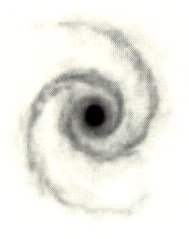

Years Before Calamity

From a narrow wooden walkway
watching clear sky moonrise

over and across tidal flow
Annisquam River lights' sheen

listening to the lap
against pilings and boat sides

wedding party music behind us
the distance before: unimaginable

dark that nearly took you
returned you

the clouds were ribbons
remember the end of the night

edge of the dock
ocean air

at home
far from home

Halibut Point
for Gary

On a wooded path to the sea,
beyond the quarry, a black butterfly
leads us to the jagged slabs of stone
that slope to water's edge. Barnacled,
the seaweed-soaked granite glistens
deep brown as wet fur. When late
afternoon light gives way to cold,
we turn back, stopping at the edge
of the quarry's deep pool to watch
the sun set. As counterpoint to chilling
air, the fiery horizon, crashing waves
silent, at a distance. In stillness
we stay through the glow. Intimate,
yet vast, the elemental touch that holds
the world, and us, together—
not in this hour alone, of course,
but this time—you tell me
what you know in every cell
is well-being, the order of things:
each, and every, in its place, in its time,
belonging. The fight goes out of you
for an hour or more. Peace, abiding,
spray of the surge, sunset, first stars,
will be forgotten again and again.
Tide going out, you take my hand.

Waiting Between Worlds

While you watched me sleep,
I felt you pick up pieces
of the life I'd lost.
The wind sounded like that,
again, tonight, ripping
the darkness, then dying
so far down the silence hurt.
I was adrift, a piece of sky
at dusk, fading, where was I?
You called my name and
I almost remembered a mother
to her child, sister to brother,
lover to lover with words
I couldn't hear clearly,
but your voice moved
inside me, gave me
direction, like rain
choosing the earth
your words fell
into me like rain.

In the Name of the Breeze

In the name of the Bee–
And of the Butterfly–
And of the Breeze–
Amen!
           Emily Dickinson

The breeze:
was it a being
present
or a wave
no beginning
no end
cooling nights
stirring dawn
a river of air
especially fresh
arrived at 10 a.m.
as if it knew you
would be waiting
on the porch
all windows
open to receive it
you welcomed
it in breathing deep
you allowed that breeze
to enter you
alive

Birch

May I call you sister, my neighbor, whose calm
at the core should be mine. I want your stillness,
the slightest rustle of feather-veined leaves
in the breeze, to be unafraid of danger, thunder
and lightning in the woods. Or do you shiver,
as I do? Growing older, I dream of slipping out
of my green dress for gold, then to be brave,
fine boned and patient in the cold. Bed of winter.
Rooted at last in something vaster than myself.
What essence passes from one life to another?
What language might we share of roots and reach,
shade and shimmer. Silver. By midsummer,
when wild roses bloom, your bark, marked
by subtle script, curls, peels back. Pages turning.

Feeding the Fire

stirs us too in our wooden boxes
low thunder of the black stove
reaches our sleep

covered in ashes
we sleep the sleep of winter
last embers under powder
dreaming of a torch

it comes a distance
carried from the summer
its blue blossom
arising in the morning

we keep the fire
its burning flower
perennial

Dublin Lake

Standing among the trees
at lake's edge, near the birch, I see
his body, also light, follows my drift

threading in and out of dark woods
so he can watch me swimming,
a ripple in the green pond.

His line cast out, a line of sight
catches my attention and I'm caught,
a catch by one also hooked.

My sheen by spring-water,
his shine by sun, we're drawn
together from where we began:

grounded—and afloat.
Both catching light
and each other's eye.

Stitches

Mei Yao Ch'en saw his wife bent over
her colored threads and bag of silk scraps,
as she did when alive, mending his clothes,
once here, then hereafter. The knotted thread
caught in his heart, in and out probed the needle,
binding them together, one hand in heaven,
the other dreaming of a seamless seam.
One thousand years since, love still finds
ways to make the ragged new. You don't
need to mend his clothes or iron his shirts.
Immaterial, the poems you write for him,
stitching you together again and again.

A Bridge
I am almost unable to bear another tragic story.

Almost: a key, a word whose weight
surpasses the others looming: *unable,
tragic, to bear* becomes a bridge
that balances before and after hearing
stories snake downstream.

The man stands on the bridge that bears
his body, his dark impulse to jump. He doesn't.
Instead, walks back the way he came—
does not stop at *unable*, hangs his hat on
almost, steps up to kiss his wife *I am.*

Arc

One cannot write about
love without calling it
something else: a glass of milk,
a boot, a cactus blooming.

It must be a cactus,
not a beach rose or a daffodil.
It must be unexpected, arising
from dry soil and flat
sleeping stems.
And then it's not just the unsought
bud or the emergence of iridescent
orange. It is each flower
rocketing forth a further blossom
from its center irresistible
in a simple arc.

The desert stretches,
curves, descends lightly
over the table by the window
in a house where marriage sits,
suns, holds itself over thin air
and radiates.
Just like that.

Peony

You could say that your lover is more
than your intimate—is the world
aching, straining against fate,
familiar, yet unrecognizable. A stranger
phased by moon and raged by fire.
Changed by rings of ice.

Broken, taken to heart and taken
in hand, the land opens, moves
aside. What does it mean
to make a life? Unfurling
from hard buds, white petals spiral,
shine open. What you once feared

has already happened, begins
the next story: the beloved,
braced for a rain of stars, guards
a circle of seeds in its radiant
house—this world of yours
holding and loving you back.

Pregnancy During a Pandemic

We talk about happiness
while the grief of nations
far exceeds the number
of its masks. But don't
say lightness of heart
is mere defense, pretense
or defiance in the face
of contagion. Rather, this
wish-made-flesh, this up-rush
of joy serious enough
takes its place in the vast
play of history and prophecy:
end-times towards—what else?
Birth. Expecting at the mercy
of everything: time, touch,
togetherness. Who will go
out too soon? Sooner or later
world wonders and fears
press in with their weight.
Counterweight. Floating
sunrise. From quiet
words blossom beyond
sorrows, dreaming
of baby names,
counting the days,
immunity for all.

The Red Thread

A young man walks into his life
to take love's hand and keeps walking.
His son holds the other hand,
when the hill appears. It could be
a storm cloud, or a wave surging
from the horizon. Still dreaming,
they climb. Days lengthen
and time shortens. Glowing red:
is it sunrise or sunset?
He can't be sure of anything
but the red thread stitching his
heart to the world, his blood
in other veins, bright buds on
branches, and in the spring grass,
the first wild strawberries.

Strawberries Under the Snow

Enveloped in fog. I seem to have no desires, no urge.
I sit beside the wood stove, the window, the bed.
Still, groceries must be bought. What does it mean
to make a *living*? We must feed ourselves, after all.
Oranges, olives, arugula. The growing season
can be measured by miles, except in the fairy tale,
where strawberries grow under the snow.
The Mediterranean fed fish to the Renaissance.
I ask you, not only how to reform the vagaries of appetite,
but what shall we feed each other?

Before I slept, a blade sliced the air beside my left cheek.
No hand held the knife, you understand.
I take it as a warning. But from whom, and against what
painful mincing of words?

Raw Materials

Say your life is straw.
Cut and dried. Gathered
into bales, kept, used
for feed, stuffing, something
to spin—but not into gold.
Do you believe in fairy tales?
In the story of an ordinary day,
the ticking of minutes' raw
material—don't believe
transformation ends
in precious metal. Art is rarely
rewarded outright. The inner life
goes back to seed over and over.
Sleeps deep. Speaks root language,
listens to earth's pulse.
Turn your life into something,
if not useful, whimsical.
Subject to wind and rain
and dawn waking the mountain
before it comes for you.
When it does, you'll wonder
whose hands were your own
and whose feet, walking the field
with a scythe, not as grim reaper
but as the instrument itself,
admiring the tall grass
before cutting it down.

Your Security has been Breached

1.
A body of water is not secure
       knows drought and flood

birds know to take refuge before the storm
       when a dark wind is rising

2.
Phishing is the new word
       for who will bite

What do they want of me

With no locks no secret code
       I lie awake and wait

3.
The body wears 4 rings (such wealth)
       Mineral - vegetable - animal - rational

and the soul wears the body

Which element of the composition
       can be stolen, can be used against me

4.
Only the heart which learns to live
       outside the body
             can sit with thieves and liars
                  and not be fooled

Content
        to slice bread
                and pour the tea

leaving crumbs
        for squirrels and winter wrens

Scarecrow in the Blessed Field
after Hildegard of Bingen's Viriditas (greening power)

God-charged
the saint calls
grass

plain green
yesterday

but waving today
and laughing!

I believe my eyes
and die a little
inside

where my old straw
hides

Bundles

My mother carried heavy bags of groceries
well into her nineties. It became harder
lugging them upstairs, but it was a matter
of principle, she felt it was hers to do.
She always called them bundles.
There are so many stories about carrying,
they weigh me down with remembering.
In one, a man comes upon an old woman
collecting firewood and offers his help.
She demands that he carry her home
with her bundle of sticks. Riding on his back,
she becomes heavier and heavier. Who
is she? What kind of a reward is that?
Carrying your little sister, your mother,
or your enemy is a choice, isn't it?
Hold on: in the dream, you can't see
whose hands tie the straps. You play
the horse, and she, the rider. Such horses
don't age, while the reins pass from one
generation to another...You find that
you like apples, don't mind being prodded
and led deeper into the world. As a matter
of principle, there is no one to blame,
no one to thank. No one puts you out
to pasture—which isn't about death,
but nibbling clover right now. Simply,
you discover you can canter for your own
pleasure. The wind feels beautiful, carries
scents of beach rose, seaweed, salt.

Fields
after A Very Common Field by Pattiann Rogers

When the field is full of tall grass,
red clover, crickets, milkweed,
and swallowtail butterflies,
you let go of naming everything—
to reach for what can't be called
and call it common. This field
appears in everyone's dreams,
so unremarkable that magical events
take place here, like rain, or the rise
of land which doesn't grow older
and evokes the games of children,
staying out late in summer to catch
lightning in a jar. Your field
is as ordinary as a body. Thriving
and dying away both at once.
While feeling a stranger
to your own form and function,
you abide in the mystery
of breath, blood and bone, the house
at the edge of the field you don't build,
but call home.

Thorndike Pond

An expert on emptiness,
measuring hours by eternity,
comes to the conclusion:
one moment is composed
of sixty-five instants,
micro-moments, if you will.
Stretch them out, as if holding
your breath underwater, to see
wonders you're skimming
over. Or, if you relax into
the depth and breadth of the full
moment, you don't need to dive.
You can find yourself at a stone
in the pond, where an old turtle,
extended from head to the end
of its dragon tail, suns itself.
Time stops. Remembers
the beginning of the world.
There, in the folds of leathery skin,
the copper shine of its thighs,
you can feel turtle-time, water
lapping rock, over and over.
You needn't count, but trust
what Dogen said must be true:
at least, 65 units of awe.

Late

    in the flight
of a heron

death of a fish

        in wind-stirred lake
        mountain peak

          breaks

to bits

   clouds too

 desiring
   to quell
     sadness

       the heart
          of the sun

       flower

what we wanted to say

    only
    heat lightning

  silence

    spoken for
    by crickets

Indra's Net

Let's remember
this hour
forever
I nearly said
dropping the words
overboard
like coins
it didn't matter
we could touch time
anyway make it ripple
our fingers trailing
new patterns
flowed out to shore
and to the mountain
our roots deep in water
even deeper in stone
leaves falling also made us
who we were
in the fabric
of the place still
echoing the eagle's cry
from the point
to another's reply
from the peak
piercing blue
circles of space
flying to its mate
twoness turned
to one and one
into too many
wings at once
as seeing
swam with a watery sun
its sparkling net
caught us
paddling home
into the mountain
shadow
for supper

Equanimity

You say writing these poems
is a waste of time, a mind-game.
But you don't hear them coming—
out of the ground, rising up,
shaken down from high branches,
falling to earth like seeds, the words
arriving. Roots, feathers and rivers,
bitter and sweet, tasted, wild
berries on the precipice you cling to.
Single notes and lines of melodies,
come looking for us looking for them
to arrange and rearrange, lift up
and set down, to choreograph
the storied sounds and shapes
side by side—to resonate in the middle
of trouble, before or after, as the cello
made to sing upon the rubble…
What if no one listens? What if
the dark tones and light, the rhythms,
beat and lyrics go unheard by anyone
but crows, or the last ones standing,
the sleepless mother, or the vast dust
cloud at the center of our galaxy
astronomers say would taste
of raspberries and smell like rum?
Why not play mind games, puzzles,
and heartstrings with all the intensity
we have and look out, after all,
with equanimity, upon the teeming
and tested, blossoming and exploding,
words coming out of the blue, white,
black, red, gold and green.

Chalice

Wave-green glass begins by fire
heat-held, melted, then of molten
flow made crystal. Listen.

Around the rim and through: it sings,
as I would to you for the goblet
full of light and lift,

if not champagne. I toast you
the base, the stem, and the bell
until stories fill its hollow

with history. Name the cup
and the blade appears: the bitter
with the sweet,

and no way to break its fall
from jeweled grail to broken bowl.
We can't recast the glass,

but we can open new windows
to water, take words
for wine.

Adam and Eve
Unfinished painting by Gustav Klimt

Before time divides
into unequal parts—no high
or low, before or after—

Eve is still at home in her skin,
and he's in her,
in paradise.

The man dreams he's safe,
at one with his lover,
but she's already left him,

communion over.
Not yet the snake
or commandment broken:

Adam's eyes are closed,
and Eve's eyes are open.

Eve Speaking

People make mistakes. First love
leads to first conflict. If we don't blame
each other, the judge on high will do it
for us. Call it conscience? Sometimes
punishment exceeds the crime. For all time.

From the beginning,
we weren't on the same page.
Take naming for example:
he calls it by shape
and I, by essence.
He counts syllables,
I like sibilance,
clicks and coos.
He sees form and function
versus life force and rhythm,
his abstract fractions against
my seasons and snakeskins.

Language is a system, a solution:
synthesis like resolution
doesn't mean we don't scratch
it out in the sand.
Patterns of wind and waves
traced on each other's skin
don't have the final word, not quite,
but serve as mnemonic device.
We also call each other names,
testing their taste: sweetheart
and darling—until we bite, spit
and growl what we need to say.

It was never easy, but I miss the early days.
It became much worse, once cursed.

Apple Tree

Once I knew nothing
but hunger and the fragrance
        of that apple.

Though small I was tall enough
to grasp the round radiant
        secret.

One bite, sweet flesh of beginnings.
Second bite, remembering the word *forbidden*,
        caught my breath and swallowed hard.

Now, I hunger
for the taste
        of paradise.

Though older, bold enough again
to pluck a burning beauty,
        secret of secrets.

One bite—naked, as in the beginning.
Second bite—ashamed by what I know and do not do.
        Third bite and more—inheritance of joys and grief

until I get to Eden's core
and what the love of wisdom needs.
        I eat the seeds.

One Light at a Time

Subtract one at a time:
traffic light,
street light,
your favorite book.
Night-light,
spot-light,
that handy flashlight.
Subtract Lucifer, the false self.
Lamp-light and torch,
the word *shine*.
Memory of dawn. Birdsong.
Subtract, one by one,
your rings. Subtract learning.
Hummingbird wings.
Take away sparklers,
fireworks, flares. You're
Eve, radiant as the day
you were made
and took the world
into your own hands.
Before you had to give
back what was given.
Eternity, flowers,
yellow ribbons. Begin
again. Still dark,
reach for matches,
and watch early
grow bright.
The day is yours,
and the words
"Let there be…"
This time light
is what you create,
the first day.

To Make Your Own Map

Start from the center or begin
at the edge and travel inward.
Every map, a mandala. Listen
for signs—birds, barks, waves
and thunder, Arvo Part's *Mirror
in Mirror* wafting from a cello.
Measure air's salt, soot, and sacrifice.
Never mind about miles. Drawing
to the scale of the soul small looms
full moon on the horizon. Name
the square where you forgot to be
a separate being. Separate yourself.
The body is its own continent. Preserve
privacy. Leave markers for posterity.
But don't include the key. Star the spot
you fell in love with a rock face. A window
in which you appeared as someone else.
Bury your expired cards and fears.
Use watercolors to blur the lines
between neighborhoods. Paint arrows
to the arts. Dedicate a park, a flock,
an ice cream stand or cone
to someone gone beyond cares.
A loved one still here
and everywhere. Get grounded.
Celebrate the spot gravity won
you over. The place you died
inside. Found the book of your dreams
or dreamed the book of your life.
Your map is interactive. Track the people
who shine, creatures who teach.
Picture how worn your ancestors'

Shoes. Don't stop to polish
your own. Cut the map into ribbons
to tie around you. The places
you've been do not define you,
but find you.

Chameleon's Manifesto

Be definite
as dew: decide to stay
then slip away

~

Rain: be sustained
for the sake of a promise
planted

~

Ring: to marry yourself
to your lover
as a bell breaks silence
to rearrange the air
above her

~

Exert reason on occasion
plain speech or oblique
and once in a while
forget to speak

The Bookshop

Some writers are clairvoyant.
More than a few. When I was twenty,
a man with enormous eyebrows
put a book in my hand. *Living Art,*
his bookshop, had shelves full
of mysteries, not murders, per se—
the occult kind. Secret societies,
astrology, Tarot. You know,
the unknowable laid bare,
here and there. No beads or incense.
It was serious. He collected the poets,
mystics, ancient and modern,
Bhagavad Gita, Tibetan Book of the Dead.
In the book he chose for me,
Posthumous Papers of George Archibald,
a writer-seer describes actual private lives—
the inevitable clear to him before it happens.
For real. Eerie, isn't it?
Who would want to live in those pages.
Writer becomes prophet,
warning the world of its demise.
Does prophesy ever change the outcome?
To read fate in faces, auras, or palms—
and write it, as chance would have it,
as fiction! Chilling. What is that?
Autobiography? Fantasy or fact?
The bookseller's eyes bore into me.
He called me a poet. Bells on his door
jangling, as I left, with my future self.

Blue Banana

The psychologist wanted to say, "Why not live? Start over? Your pain will subside; you can meet somebody new."

Instead, he asked the man if he remembered his dreams.

A blue banana?

Not knowing how to comfort the man in his great loneliness, he said, "Let's talk about it next time."

Then the sky, in love with the world, began to paint everything blue.

The Hiker
after the painting by Joan Hanley

You keep thinking of one boy in a blue jacket.
He could be your friend, or your son, or your son's
friend, or a young man you wanted but never found
when you were twenty, or thirty, or more. Bending
over his cellphone, the intense blue sky over him,
behind him the dark sea, he must be searching
for an answer. If he consults the oracle, Siri
will say this place does not exist on any map.
Clouds build, shedding opals mid-sky. Such stillness,
you stop whatever you're doing. Stop getting older.
Cease complaining and wanting and even praising
falls silent. Calm, before the storm, as if an earthquake,
as if a tsunami wasn't possible, as if the great
wave of uncertainty wasn't at your back too,
eerie and bleak and beautiful. Inhale, count one,
two, three, four, five; hold, and let it go as the tide
pulls back from the shore. When the young man
looks up, it will feel as if you've always been there
together. You could offer a hand, a way, a list
of which paths not to take. But he's already
following his intuition. For all you know, he's not
on google maps but texting the love of his life.

The Art of Falling

Everything set against a country
of chasms.

In the dream you don't see
the voice that moves you
but take to heart its promise
everything will be all right.
So you step off.

Nothing grandiose
no spreading of wings
no arrogance
but simple faith
in falling.

Down and down the rich green sides
on the way you know
strangely calm
there is no possible way
to survive—

But maybe the art of falling
includes a perfect landing.
Might you find your footing after all?
Last straws fall away

in the plunge. Deeper still
you resign yourself
to death
with the decision
to find it interesting
this secret to living
dying.

Magnetic Storm

Over snow   flashes beyond moonlight
solar flares make the sky pulse

Watching from a night field
in wind my pulse keeps time
or fear

where bare trees bend in the tide
that shakes me too
attached to which branch

My family had no prayers
I made my own
Years gust and pass   I want to say

pray with me
I have not seen heaven
signal like this

~

On the snowmobile trail
   we sink up to our knees laughing
The gale makes us feel small   I am the smallest

and hold onto my friends not to be blown over
   I have come to watch and won't lose my ground
New Hampshire hilltop that has been home

before I leave here I will read the space around you
   and there it flares! Of course I learn
to scan the whole sky even the moon alert

to what the long arm of the sun stirs up
    Our little powers flicker

~

Animals pass through the wind
waiting to reappear
We think they are gone

But what do we know
of how spirit moves over the land
at a time like this preparing

spring   Sensing what can't be seen
we tremble
and turn back to the house

~

To stay
grounded
I kneel

like a stunted pine
high up clinging
to stone
not to break

My shadow
punctuates
moonlight on blue snow

~

Later we drink tea from lemon balm passion flower
and mugwort to help us remember our snow dreams
What we talked about out of the wind

was leaving Abbot Hill soon
and how after our young student died suddenly
we could still feel her close to this land and sky

The eagle appeared three times
twice in the cards
then flying where no one expected

like one of the names for grief
charging the field
as what electric love we have flares forth

Finger Painting

First picture a sun rising in the body of your enemy.
It may be an angry sun at first, stamped or smudged
with a red fingerprint.
It will feel like winter all over again. Fire
on the hearth consuming itself, leaving
black ribbons, charred wands, a chill in the heart.

When night's shadow falls like a tree
across the hands buried in your lap,
adapt to a low ceiling—go starless.
Every species that ever lived has been betrayed.
Thousands of years of disappointments
shrink or stretch us. Someone's bitter thumbprint—
an eclipse of the moon.

A sun is rising in the interior
of more than seven billion bodies—eyes
look out at us from their birth. Irises blue,
violet, green, and brown. The whites milky and mild.
Pride gives us silver pieces to spend in the spinning galaxy.
But the remedy for hate is to paint a sun rising
in the breast of your enemy. And then, to sleep.

Brush Work

Some nights we climb into landscape paintings
Chinese sages made from aged ink

to lose ourselves between the peaks.
But we're from the west and Plato says art is nothing

but imitation of imitation…
while elation in the real is found only in ideal

forms. Ideas. No wonder we want what they
found at the bottom of their cups. Not leaves alive

but left for dead having made the liquid living.
Wild words soaked in sweet rice wine

or bitter brine still giving what we need to taste.
The moon's shadow crossed the sun today.

Art is not easy. The ink-dark circle made a perfect
fit. Calligraphy's brush is made from goats, sheep,

horses, wolves, weasel, marten and sometimes cats.
Or rabbits. People cheered when the light returned,
and then went back to work.

Chauvet Cave
after the film Cave of Forgotten Dreams

We step, you and I, with the cameraman,
into the room of our ancestors
where the painter left a handprint in red ochre.
Bodies of lions, cave bears, two rhinos with horns locked
were drawn from the contours of cave walls, sketched
in charcoal on stone scraped clean.
After centuries fixed in the dark—horses stir
again, sniff the air and stamp the ground.
Without a ritual fire, without a story
of the hunt, without knowing what god moved
the hand to sketch a woman's pelvis and crown
her with the head of a bison, with nothing
but these cavernous halls and a scattering
of bones, we wake to animals in torch light
living our vivid dreams of wind and hunger.

~

You may look up from the page or the screen
to the hills, eroding, clear cut, and wonder
about making a mark, leaving an impression…
and then pull back from that train of thought,
with its inevitable conclusions. To leap,
Darwin says, is not predictable, but improvisation.
And you and I thought change would slow
down as we aged. As the universe ought to curb
its expansion and slow down, for God's sake,
start reversing direction, return (almost)
endlessly back on itself towards its origin—
to reassemble the pieces of creation by magnetic
pull back to *the* north, *the* homing, but no.

We grow and grow the terrible knowledge
of ourselves. We want, while fading, to glow.
We go on. And what will we send back?
Like stars now extinguished that still look like
they're burning, what words could reach
beyond us? Or more to the point:
what will we ray forward from this cave
of the mind into the new?
The idea of a gesture, or
the hand itself already moving
beyond the flames.

Ideal Company

Our daughter wants to talk about Plato.
This is the best hour—we will look back one day
and remember the ideal dialogue, as sunlight
makes leaf shadows on the wall. What do we know
we don't know? Each idea a steppingstone. We pick
up the smoothest rocks, the most beautiful, the cracked,
the fool's gold. Still no philosopher's stone. Who can
reach deep, or high enough to remember the gleam
of first forms? Our lips give thanks for the good life
before closing around fresh, yellow pears. Then we try
to think about fig-ness. Could it be any more purple than these?

Fresh Figs

Ripening goes slowly at first,
you were eager to feel
at your peak, but now—
suddenly succulent, lavishly
sweet—intimate enough
with the world to be taken,
enjoyed, swallowed entire—
are you happy or sad,
afraid to give yourself
away? Or too fulfilled
to care—when lifted
to a face you can't but love,
all the earth made of you,
perfume the breeze
carries away.

Peonies, a Bouquet

A contagion
        of letting go

spring bowing out
        to summer

bleeding petals
        a signal

from one stem
        to another

giving way
        to a party

of the end
        ever after!

I gathered them
        like lost children

to rest
        beneath the trees

there was a lightness
        to the moment

I didn't feel
        one purple petal fell

on the white porcelain sink
        in the shape of a heart

At the End of the Dying Day

Listening to the bird
nearest the heart
in its cradle of pine
swaddled by sunlight
a canopy of emerald
we feel we are close
to beginning the end
and wait for what comes
to defy reason—
the coracle of the soul
a shell empty
of its swimmer
all liquid for a season
until dripping lake water
on rough sand
we discover the loons
have left for the dark
sea—left us alone
to make amends
to the land and beings
we have undone
all but the voices
rearranged by wind
into something other
than we know—
when whatever flows
begins to go away
even daylight gets smaller
watch the horizon
as it sets behind one
mountain quietly
changing its shape
feather by feather

Here

        among miles of heather
                purple red orange burnt orange
stretching over the highlands in Scotland

 there   in the peace of no bird
        no rustling thing   no silent deer   all alone
             I ask God to speak to me

and in the silence
             what does God say
                                nothing

          the most powerful
     absence
          miles of heather all around   no bird no
  sound   even the silent deer are   nowhere
           and I say God   can you speak to me
     then of course I listen with might
                  and expectation empties

when no other voice says

        I am here

I Would Like to Be a Friend of Silence

Cultivate quiet, swallow
words that aren't ripe for saying,
learn unspoken languages,
and spell out the meanings of moss, metal,
stone and stream. Sipping tea, the life
of leaf, flower, and seed upon my tongue,
I want to tell you I've found the recipe
for kindness, the solution to a problem,
the source of a wild will to live—but
you're not here. Without you near,
I practice keeping words to myself,
but for silence, if she's listening.

Patrice Pinette received her MFA from Vermont College of Fine Arts. In the Connections Program of New Hampshire Humanities, she facilitates book discussions with adult learners of English from all over the world. She also leads poetry workshops in the Transdisciplinary Studies in Healing Education program at Antioch University New England, and Center for Anthroposophy's Renewal Courses. Patrice's poems have appeared in literary journals and anthologies including Pensive: A Global Journal of Spirituality & the Arts, Touchstone Journal, Poet Showcase: An Anthology of New Hampshire Poets, Allegro Poetry Journal, Hampden-Sydney Poetry Review, and elsewhere.

ACKNOWLEDGMENTS

Adanna Journal, "When my First Husband Made Another Woman Pregnant"

Connecticut River Review, "Fantasy Bites the Tail of the Living"

COVID Spring: Granite State Pandemic Poems, "Pregnancy During a Pandemic"

Evening Street Review, "Chauvet Cave," "Dark Energy"

Flash!Point, "Venus on Holiday"

Hampden-Sydney Poetry Review, "As If"

Images from Ruin, "The World"

Inflectionist Review, "Blue Door"

Migrations and Home, "Choreography," "Magnetic Storm"

Northern New England Review, "Down from Temple Mountain"

Pensive: A Global Journal of Spirituality & the Arts, "Blue is a Being," "Equanimity"

Poet Showcase: An Anthology of New Hampshire Poets, "Here"

Touchstone Journal, "Don't Hate Winter," "Impulse," "One Light at a Time," "Halibut Point"

Smoky Quartz, "Finger Painting"

Snapdragon Journal of Art and Healing, "Anima Mundi," "Waiting Between Worlds"

Writing the Land, "Birch"

GRATITUDES

Deep thanks to my talented friends, artists and writers, who devoted precious time and attention to help bring this book into being: Alice B Fogel, Thomas Moore, Joan Hanley, and Emily Archer.

Many thanks to Karine Munk Finser for including my poetry workshops and readings in the visionary programs she directs, and to Paul Matthews, one of my earliest guides in the realm of imaginative writing and teaching.

To other friends who have taken my poems to heart and shared their own creative practice, enhancing mine: Candace Bergstrom, Enid Ames, Carol Renwick, Blake Wood, Beverly Boyer, Craig Milewski, and Arthur Auer—abiding thanks.

Endless gratitude to my mother for her belief in me, her generosity, and her loving spirit. Heartfelt thanks to my sister Susan whose sensitivity and insight helped some of these poems come to fruition.

To my daughter Ariana and my son Jonah—your presence in my life is the greatest gift. To my husband Gary—thank you for supporting me beyond measure and for cherishing my voice.

To Mike Nelson and Bee Monk Press—thank you for transforming my manuscript into this book.

Copyright © 2025 by Patrice Pinette
ISBN: 9798302568007
P.O. Box 110, New Durham, NH. 03855
beemonkpress.com
beemonkpress@gmail.com

Made in United States
North Haven, CT
28 January 2025